Ribbons & Threads

Baltimore Style

Bonnie K. Browning

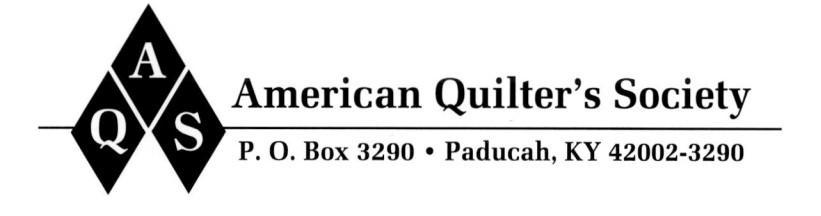

American Quilter's Society
P. O. Box 3290 • Paducah, KY 42002-3290

Located in Paducah, Kentucky, the American Quilter's Society (AQS), is dedicated to promoting the accomplishments of today's quilters. Through its publications and events, AQS strives to honor today's quiltmakers and their work – and inspire future creativity and innovation in quiltmaking.

Book Design & Illustrations – Whitney Hopkins
Cover Design – Karen Chiles
Photography – Charles R. Lynch

Library of Congress Cataloging-in-Publication Data

Browning, Bonnie, 1944–
    Ribbons & threads : Baltimore Style / Bonnie K. Browning.
       p.   cm.

    Includes bibliographical references (p.).
    ISBN 0-89145-897-2
    1. Patchwork. 2. Silk ribbon embroidery. 3. Miniature quilts.
4. Album quilts--Maryland--Baltimore. I. Title.
TT835.B74   1996
746.46'041--dc21   96-49792
                                                                                        CIP

American Quilter's Society,
P.O. Box 3290, Paducah, KY 42002-3290
http://www.AQSquilt.com

Copyright: 1996, Bonnie K. Browning
$14.95

This book or any part thereof may not be reproduced without the written consent of the author and publisher. The information and patterns in this book have been provided in good faith. The American Quilter's Society has no control of materials or methods used, and therefore is not responsible for the use of or results obtained from this information.

Dedication

To my husband,
Wayne,
who always supports my quilting, my travels,
and has fun with me along the way;
and
to my mother,
Mary Kirkland,
who taught me to sew,
to enjoy handwork and crafts;
and who instilled in me
that I could do anything I wanted to do.
Thanks, Mom!

Acknowledgments

Special thanks go to:

Meredith Schroeder, whose love of quilting is illustrated by her dedication to today's quilters; and who encourages me to put my quiltmaking knowledge on paper;

the many quilting instructors that I have studied with over the years; mine is a collective knowledge because of you;

the students who take my classes; it is such great fun to see you stretch your wings; and,

my friends, Lois Arnold, Linda Braun, Peggy Greene, JoAnn Lischynski, Phyllis Miller, Peggy Morrison, Janet Myers, Marie Salazar, Anita Shackelford, and Ruth Ann Thompson, with whom I bounce ideas and learn new things; you inspire me and make sure I get some quilting done.

Contents

- Introduction 5
- Supplies 6
- Fabric 7
- Stitches 9
- General Directions 15
- The Blocks 16
    - Block 1 – Ruched Rose 16
    - Block 2 – Berry Wreath 17
    - Block 3 – Eight-Petal Rose Wreath 18
    - Block 4 – Cherry Wreath 19
    - Block 5 – Rose Wreath 20
    - Block 6 – Wild Rose Wreath 21
    - Block 7 – Rose Garden Wreath 22
    - Block 8 – Heart Rosebud Wreath 23
    - Block 9 – Grapes & Roses 24
- Embroidered Vine Border 25
- Quilted Feather Vine Border 25
- Finishing the Quilt 29
- References 31
- About the Author 31

Introduction

The Baltimore album quilts intrigue me, and it takes many, many hours to complete a large album quilt. By using silk ribbon, embroidery stitches, and designs common to these beautiful mid-nineteenth century quilts, I am able to make a miniature Baltimore style quilt with three-dimensional flowers in a small fraction of the time an appliquéd quilt takes to stitch.

Gardening, especially flowers, is one of my hobbies. I love roses, whether they are the wild ones like those that grow in the state of Iowa where I grew up, or the groomed single long-stemmed rose that my husband surprises me with from time to time that says "I love you." It seems very appropriate that my little Baltimore style quilt should be titled, "Smitten with Flowers."

Some of the design elements used repeatedly in the Baltimore album quilts are bouquets, baskets of fruits and flowers, wreaths in circular and heart shapes, X-shaped floral blocks, and trailing vines. You'll find several traditional blocks in this quilt and others of my own original design.

Baltimore album quilts often use techniques such as appliqué and reverse appliqué, piecing, stuffed work, cording, and embroidery. By using silk ribbon and embroidery stitches, that intricate detail can be achieved by taking only a few stitches.

In a quilt containing multiple borders, one or more of them would often be of whitework. In "Smitten with Flowers," the quilted, undulating feather border repeats the shape of the embroidered grapes and floral border.

As you work through each of the nine blocks and borders of this quilt, you will learn 17 different embroidery stitches to be worked in either thread or ribbon. I challenge you to take the lessons you learn here to make the next generation of quilts in your own style.

Bonnie Browning

Supplies

20" square of 100% white cotton fabric for background, plus 1" x 72" bias strip for binding

20" square backing fabric

20" square lightweight batting (a split layer of poly/cotton batting makes a good filler)

The variegated silk ribbons vary considerably from one batch to the next, so try to purchase the amount you need at one time if you want it to be consistent.

4mm silk ribbon: (Specific colors of ribbons and threads used in cover quilt are in parentheses)
- 3 yds. variegated red for flowers (Poinsettia)
- 3 yds. yellow/red orange for flowers (Snap Dragon)
- 3 yds. variegated violet/gold (Dutch Iris)
- 3 yds. variegated green I for leaves (Holly)
- 3 yds. variegated green II for leaves (Rain Forest)
- 3 yds. variegated green III for leaves (Ivy)
- 6 yds. variegated green for border (Holly)

7mm silk ribbon:
- 3 yds. blue/blue green for folded roses (Sea Weed)
- 3 yds. variegated green for leaves (Rain Forest)

THREAD:
- 1 skein red silk embroidery thread for berries (Madeira #0511)
- 3 skeins green silk embroidery thread for stems (1 each Madeira #1312, #1314 & #1508)
- 1 skein gold silk embroidery thread for flower centers (Madeira #2211)
- 1 skein white silk embroidery thread for block and border outlines (Madeira White)
- 1 spool #8 purple perle cotton for grapes (you could also use two strands of purple silk embroidery thread)
- Sewing or embroidery threads to match ribbons
- Quilting thread to match background fabric

NEEDLES:
- #22 or #24 chenille needles for ribbon
- #7 embroidery needles for threads
- quilting needles
- 14" quilting hoop

Note: Test your ribbons for colorfastness by wetting one end of a ribbon and blotting it between white paper towels. If any color is transferred to the towel, rinse the ribbon in clear water until the water is free of any color. Line dry and press.

Please be sure to do this test of your ribbon. Do as I say and not as I did! When the quilting was nearly complete on "Smitten," water on the quilt caused one of the red ribbons to run. That resulted in having to carefully remove the ribbons and threads in two blocks of the quilt without damaging the fabric. The dye stains had to be removed, and the two blocks had to be re-stitched. Doing all of the stitching from the top of the quilt while hiding the ends and traveling stitches was no small feat. Hopefully my lesson will save you from the trauma I went through as I saw that red color gradually bleeding onto my quilt. Some brands of ribbon bleed, while others do not. Test to be sure!

Fabric

PREPARING THE FABRIC

Wash and dry the fabric before cutting it to size to allow for any shrinkage.

Cut the top 20" square; this extra fabric will make it possible to put the entire quilt in a hoop without smashing the ribbon flowers and leaves.

Find the center point of the square by folding it in half, and then in half again. Finger press the center point; from this center point, measure 1⅞" above the center point, using the edge of the square as a guide to keep the line straight, and draw a line with a disappearing fabric marker or lightly with a pencil. Draw the next line 3¾" from the first line. Continue drawing until you have created nine 3¾" blocks centered on the fabric square. Draw a square 1" from the outside perimeter of the nine blocks for the embroidered border. Finally, draw a square 1½" from the edges of the previous border (this is the outside edge of the quilt).

If you used a disappearing marker (and I did), you will want to stitch basting threads over your marked lines. If you do this and are interrupted from your stitching, the lines will be marked with thread.

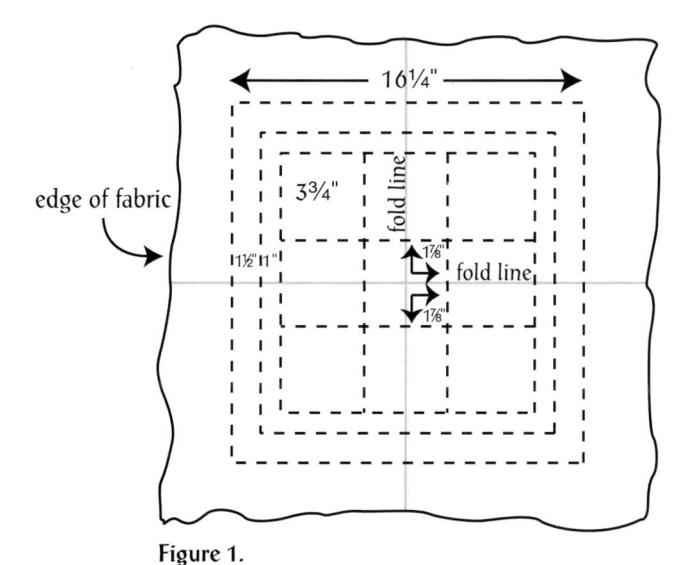

Figure 1.

USING A ROUND HOOP

Using a round hoop to stitch and quilt makes the project very portable. If your hoop will not hold a single layer of fabric good and taut, you may need to wrap the inside ring with strips of muslin to give a better grip. The "No Slip" hoop keeps a single layer of fabric taut without wrapping the inner ring.

Adjust the screw on the frame of the hoop so the outer ring fits easily over the inner ring. Place the marked fabric over the inner ring. Press the outer ring down over the fabric (Fig. 2). The grain of the fabric should be straight and taut. Do not tighten the fabric by pulling on the fabric; this will distort the weave of the fabric. If you need to adjust the fabric, loosen the screw, remove the outer ring, adjust the fabric, and replace the outer ring.

Use this same procedure for embroidering the top and for quilting the layers together. It is very tempting to just pull on the edges of the fabric to tighten it. If you take a few extra seconds to remove the ring and adjust the fabric, you will not risk causing distortion in your project.

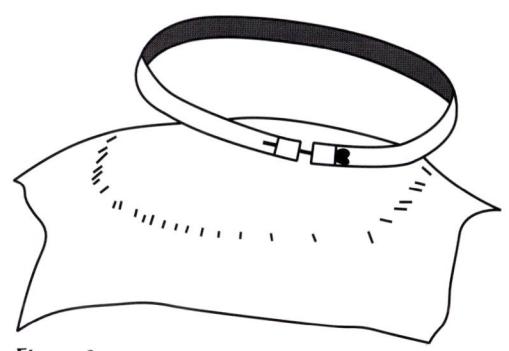

Figure 2.

STITCHING THE BLOCKS & BORDERS OUTLINE

Place the quilt top in a round hoop. Use a single strand of white silk embroidery thread to Cable Stitch the outlines of the nine blocks and on both sides of the embroidered border. Stitch the lines marked in Fig. 1.

When the outline is complete, you are ready to mark the guidelines for stitching each block.

MARKING THE BLOCKS

The individual blocks are marked with only a few positioning marks. Draw the stem line and mark only the position of the flowers, leaves, and buds. The blocks will be stitched in the same order that a flower

Ribbons & Threads: Baltimore Style

grows – first the stems, then leaves, and finally the flowers. One exception (and there always seems to be at least one exception) is stitching the Rosebud. When the bud is encased in two small leaves, the bud is stitched first and the two leaves overlap at the base of the rosebud.

NEEDLES

The barrel of the needle must create a hole large enough for the ribbon to pass through. If the ribbon does not pass through the fabric easily, a larger needle is needed. The ribbon should lay flat in the eye of the needle.

THREADING THE NEEDLE WITH RIBBON

Slip one end of the ribbon through the eye of the needle (Fig. 3).

Pick up one end of the ribbon and push the needle through the center of the ribbon, about ⅜" from the end. Pull the long tail of ribbon until the short tail is at the eye of the needle. Using this threading method allows you to stitch through the fabric with a single ribbon.

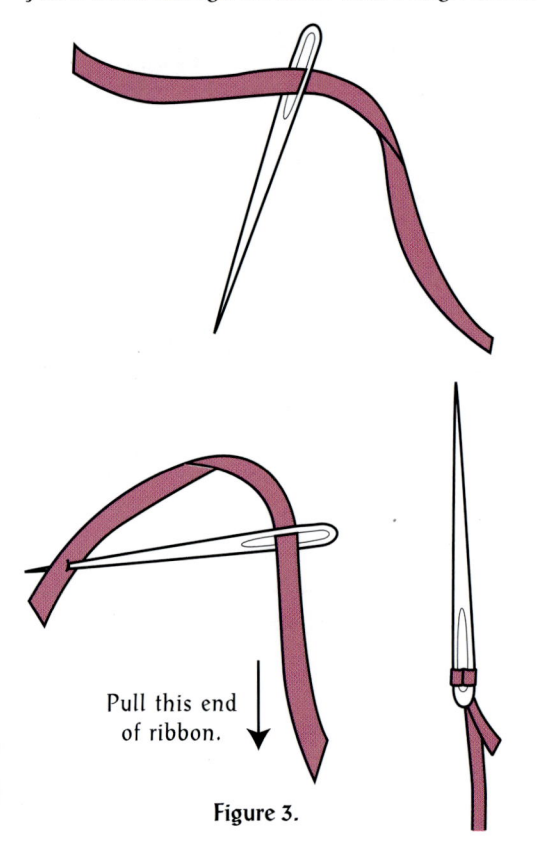

Pull this end of ribbon.

Figure 3.

KNOTTING THE RIBBON

To knot the end of the ribbon, fold the end of the ribbon over about ⅜" and insert the needle in the center of the ribbon through both layers (Fig. 4). Take hold of the ⅜" end and pull the ribbon toward the eye of the needle; pull the needle until the soft knot forms at the end of the ribbon.

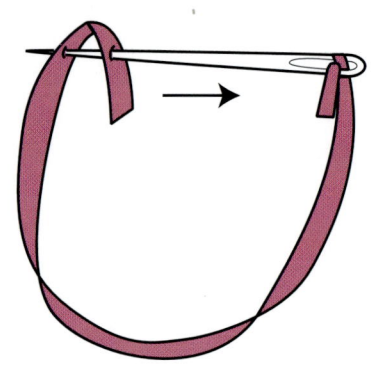

Figure 4.

KNOT TO END STITCHING

Push the needle and ribbon through to the back side of the fabric. Slide the needle under a stitch and take a backstitch through the ribbon. It helps to hold the ribbon you are stitching through with your finger or thumb so you do not disturb the stitches on the right side of the fabric. Take another backstitch to lock the first one. Cut the ribbon close to the last stitch.

Stitches

This section provides, in alphabetical order for easy reference, all of the embroidery stitches used in this project. These stitches can be used for stitching with embroidery threads or silk ribbons. The stitches used for each block are indicated with the block pattern.

BACKSTITCH

Backstitching with thread is used for thin stems and lettering.

Bring needle up at B, a short distance from the starting point.

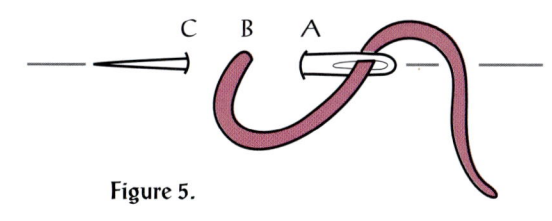

Figure 5.

Take needle down at A, the starting point.

Bring needle up at C, the same distance as the A to B backstitch (Fig. 5).

Continue stitching in this manner.

CABLE STITCH

The Cable Stitch is used to outline the nine 3" blocks and on both edges of the embroidered border.

Bring needle up at A.

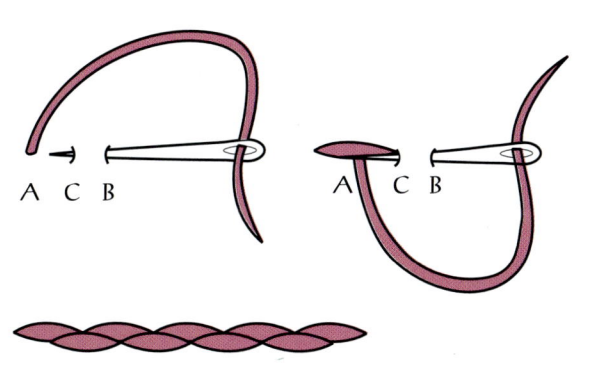

Figure 6.

Insert needle the desired stitch length from A and take needle down at B, keeping the thread above the needle, and come up at C.

Work the next stitch on your marked line, but switch the thread below the needle (Fig. 6).

Continue stitching on the line, alternating the thread above and below the needle.

CENTER-GATHERED ROSE

The Center-Gathered Roses are quick and easy to make. They look like 'real' roses.

Cut 3" of 4mm silk ribbon for each Center-Gathered Rose. Thread a needle with thread matching the ribbon; knot one end of the thread.

Fold one end under ¼", form a circle with the ribbon, placing the other cut end under the folded end so the cut ends of the ribbon are aligned (Fig. 7). Stitch close to the folded edge. Knot the thread; do not cut it off yet.

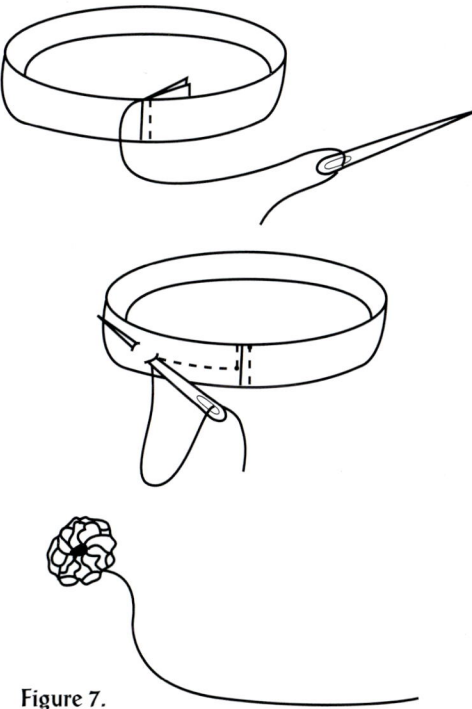

Figure 7.

Stitch a running stitch in the center of the ribbon all the way around.

Pull the thread to gather the rose. Take a couple of stitches across the bottom of the rose to secure. Knot the thread and leave the thread attached to sew the rose to the quilt (Fig. 7).

Ribbons & Threads: Baltimore Style

CHAIN STITCH

The basic Chain Stitch makes loops shaped like teardrops and can be used for flower petals, leaves, or thicker stems and vines.

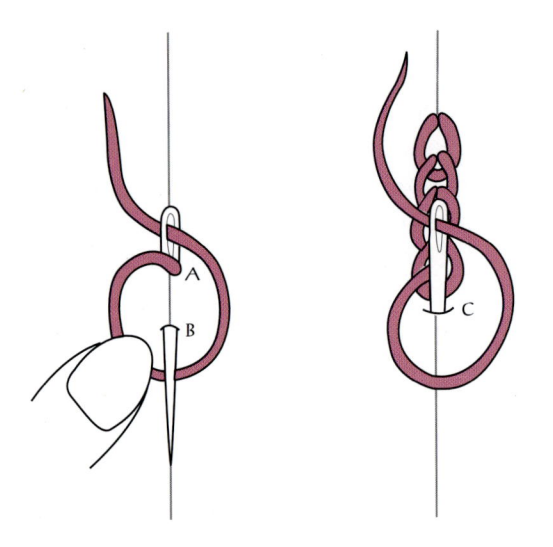

Figure 8.

Bring needle up at A (Fig. 8).
Take needle down at the same point (A).
Form a loop and hold it in place with your thumb.
Bring the needle up at B and place it over the thread.
Pull needle through to form a single Chain Stitch.
Insert needle at C, making a small stitch to secure the Chain Stitch.

For leaves, pull the chain so center is nearly closed. Flower petals will be looser and more open.

COLONIAL KNOT

The Colonial Knot sits flatter than a French Knot and makes a good center for flowers or single small berries.

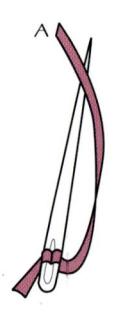

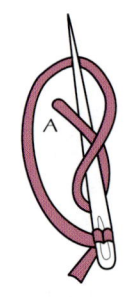

Figure 9.

Figure 10.

Bring the needle up at A.
Slide the needle to the right under the ribbon.
Grasp the ribbon, pulling the ribbon over and then under the needle to form a figure eight (Fig. 9).
With the needle vertical, insert the needle close to, but not in, the original hole (Fig. 10).
Slide the knot down to the fabric before pulling the thread through.

CORAL STITCH

The Coral Stitch consists of small knots, which can be spaced close together or far apart. Spaced approximately ⅛" apart, a line of Coral Stitches looks like rose stems with thorns.

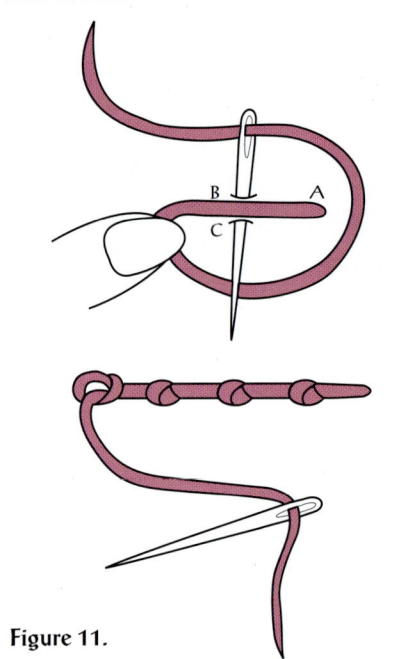

Figure 11.

Bring needle up at A (Fig. 11).
Lay thread along stitching line and hold in place with your thumb.

Ribbons & Threads: Baltimore Style

Take a stitch under the thread, down at B and up at C.

Loop thread under the needle.

Pull thread through forming a knot.

EDGE-GATHERED ROSE

The Edge-Gathered Roses are fun and easy to make. Other types of flowers can be made using this technique by adding French Knots or French Knots on a Stalk for flower centers.

Cut 4" of 4mm silk ribbon for each Edge-Gathered Rose.

Thread a needle with thread matching the ribbon; knot one end.

Fold one end of the ribbon ¼" and form a circle with the ribbon, placing the other cut end under the folded end so the cut ends of the ribbon are aligned. Stitch close to the folded edge. Knot the thread; do not cut it off yet (Fig. 12).

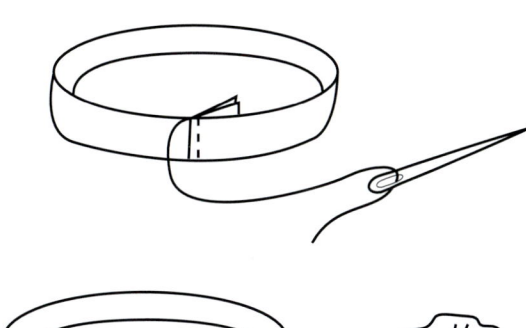

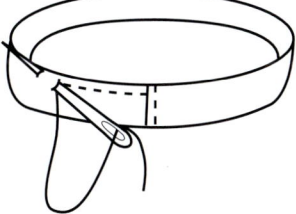

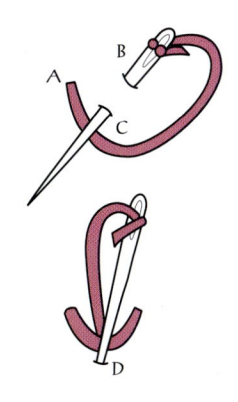

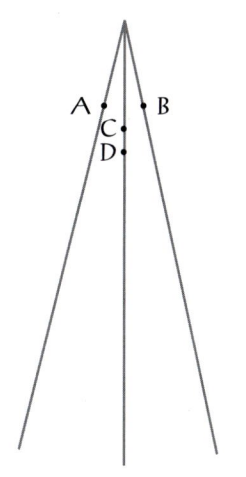

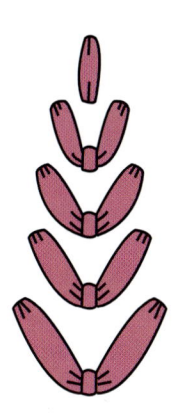

Figure 12.

Figure 13.

Stitch a running stitch along one edge of the ribbon, going around the entire circle.

Pull up the thread to gather the rose. Take 2 or 3 stitches across the bottom of the rose and knot the thread. Leave the thread attached to sew the rose to the background fabric.

FLY STITCH

The Fly Stitch is used to make leaves on an embroidered stem. You can change the spacing, length, and arrangements of all parts of the stitch for added variety.

Bring the needle up at A (Fig. 13).

Take it down at B and up at C; the thread should be under the needle.

Pull the needle through and take a small stitch, down at D, to anchor the loop.

FOLDED ROSE

The Folded Rose is made by folding ribbon. Once you've mastered the technique, you'll be able to make several in a few minutes.

Thread a needle with thread matching the ribbon; knot one end.

From 7mm ribbon, fold 6" from one end at a right angle; leave the ribbon attached to your whole length of ribbon (Fig. 14, on page 12). You'll see why in a minute.

Fold the bottom ribbon up and to the left.

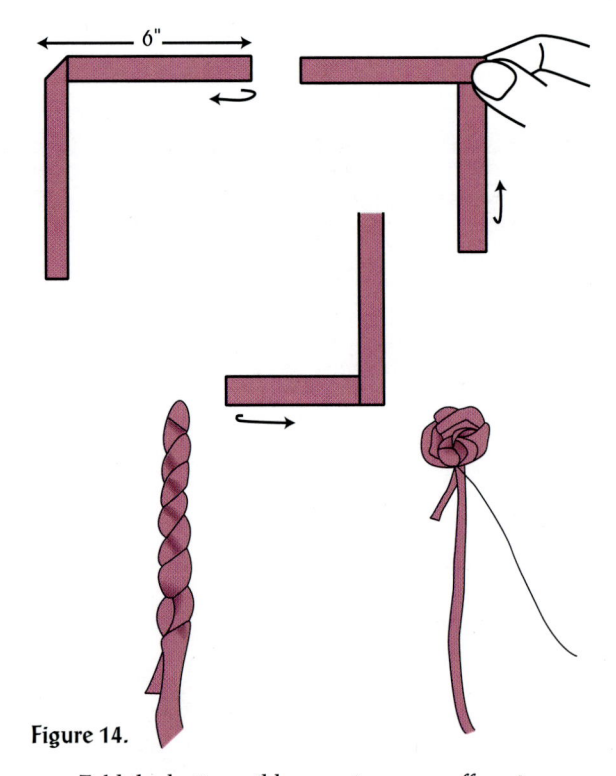

Figure 14.

Fold the bottom ribbon up to square off again.

Continue folding until there is just enough ribbon left to hold onto in one hand.

Holding onto both ends of the ribbon, release the folded ribbon; it will spring out like an accordion. Pull the longer end of the ribbon (the one you did not cut off) and watch the rose form.

Push the threaded needle from the top down through the center of the rose. Take 2 or 3 stitches up and down through the rose, ending with the thread on the bottom. Wrap the tails of the rose several times with thread, knot, and leave the thread attached. You'll use this thread to sew the rose to the background fabric.

By not cutting off your ribbon initially, you will save a considerable amount of ribbon if you are making several Folded Roses.

FRENCH KNOT

French Knots are good to use for flower centers, berries, or cherries.

Bring needle up at the point you want the knot.

Wind the thread around the needle once or twice (Fig. 15).

Pull the thread taut but not tight on the needle and insert needle close to the starting point.

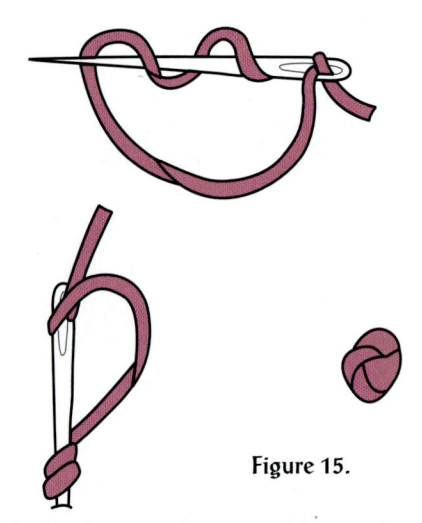

Figure 15.

Slide the thread down to the fabric and pull needle through the loop.

Several French Knots can fill the center of a flower.

For a rounded, neater knot, use a thicker thread and one twist around the needle.

FRENCH KNOT ON A STALK

You can vary the flower centers by making a French Knot on a Stalk. Instead of taking the needle down close to the starting point as you did in making the French Knot, take it down a short distance away (Fig. 16).

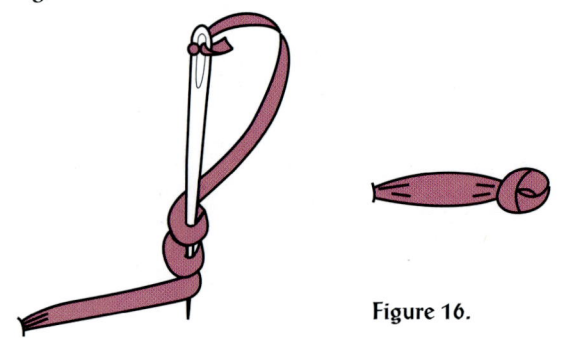

Figure 16.

RIBBON STITCH

The Ribbon Stitch is used for flower petals and leaves. The flowers can be varied by using different widths of ribbons.

Bring needle up at A (Fig. 17, page 13).

Lay the ribbon flat and insert the needle at B in the center of the ribbon.

Pull the needle through; the ribbon will curl in on both sides and form a point.

When you pull the ribbon, be careful not to pull too hard. Try placing your finger on the stitch as you

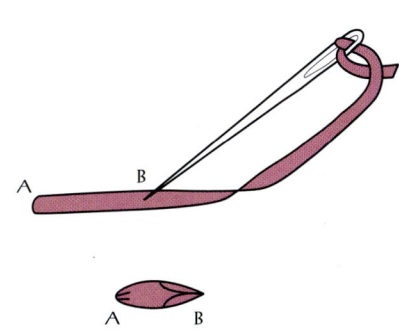

Figure 17.

pull the ribbon to avoid pulling it through the fabric. If you pull the stitch through, go back and stitch again over the top of the first one. No one will know a second stitch is there!

ROSEBUDS

Rosebuds are made using a Padded Straight Stitch for the bud and Side Ribbon Stitches for the leaves at the base.

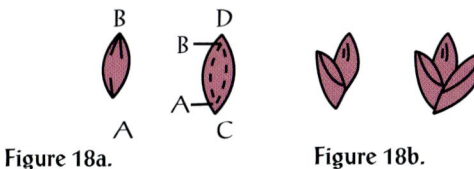

Figure 18a.   Figure 18b.

To make the Rosebud, take one Straight Stitch (Fig. 18a). Bring the needle up at A and down at B. Take a second stitch slightly longer than the first, coming over the first one, bringing needle up at C and down at D. This is a Padded Straight Stitch.

To make the leaves, add a Side Ribbon Stitch to each side of the bud (Fig. 18b).

RUCHED ROSE

The Ruched Rose is made from a single piece of silk ribbon and can be made any size you wish, from a beautiful single open rose using 4mm ribbon, to smaller roses and buds using 2mm ribbon.

Cut a 15" piece of 4mm ribbon. Fold each end at a 45° angle, pin in place (Fig. 19). Using a single strand of silk embroidery thread to match the ribbon, begin stitching in a zigzag pattern across the ribbon. Because the ribbon is fragile, only about 4 stitches across the ribbon are needed to gather it easily. As you stitch, gather the ribbon occasionally and continue stitching across the length of the ribbon. After the entire length of ribbon has been stitched and gathered, make a knot to secure the ruching in place. Your ruched ribbon should be approximately 4" long. Keep the thread attached; you will use it to attach the rose to the background.

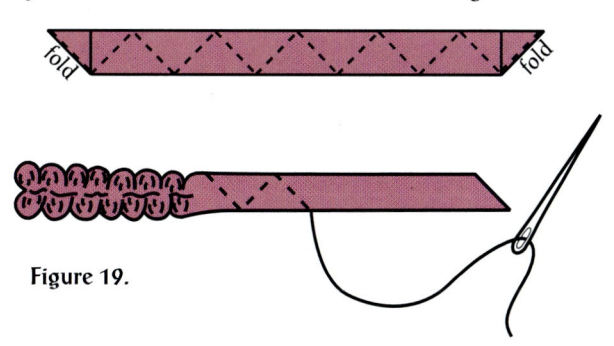

Figure 19.

Lightly draw a ¾" circle on the background fabric in the location you want the Ruched Rose. To stitch the ruched piece to the background, begin by tacking the ruched ribbon on the outside of the circle with the center of the ribbon lined up with the drawn circle (Fig. 20). Continue wrapping the ruched ribbon around, forming the open rose, with the end tucked in the center. Be sure to tack the ribbon securely in place as you form the Ruched Rose.

Figure 20.

SIDE RIBBON STITCH

The Side Ribbon Stitch adds variety to leaves and petals, making the sides roll similarly to the way real leaves would. It is also used to make leaves at the base of a Rosebud.

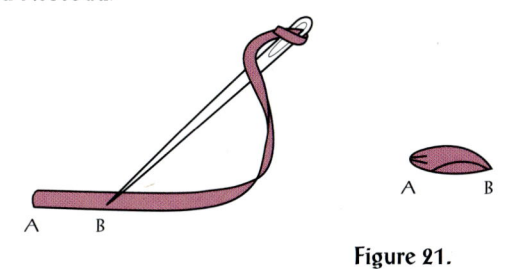

Figure 21.

Bring needle up at A (Fig. 21).

Lay ribbon flat and insert the needle at B, near the edge of the ribbon.

Ribbons & Threads: Baltimore Style

Pull the needle through; the ribbon will curl over to one side.

STEM STITCH

This stitch forms a smooth, rope-like line that is often used for flower stems and vines. It can be thin or thick, depending on the angle at which the needle is inserted.

It is important to always bring the needle up on the same side of the stitching line. When working a curve, bring the needle up on the inside; the thread will rest above your needle as you stitch.

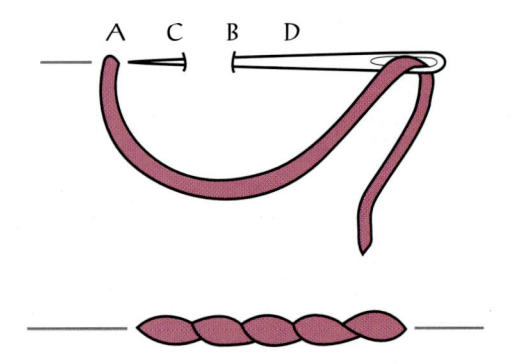

Figure 22.

Bring the needle up at A (Fig. 22).

Insert needle down at B.

Bring needle up at C, halfway between A and B.

Insert needle down at D, making stitches the same length.

For a thicker stem, stitch across the line rather than along the line.

STRAIGHT STITCH

The Straight Stitch can be used for buds, petals, and leaves.

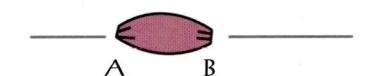

Figure 23a.

Bring the needle up at A and take it down at B the desired distance (length of the petal) (Fig. 23a).

Mark a Straight Stitch flower by drawing a circle for the outer edge of the flower (Fig. 23b). Draw a Y and fill in two additional petals equidistant each side of the Y.

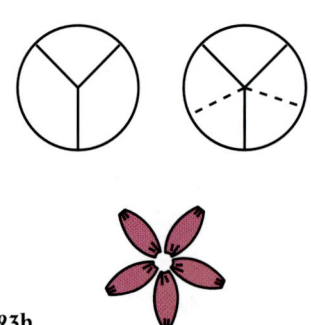

Figure 23b.

To avoid having so many stitches in the center of the flower, start each petal close to, but not in, the center of the flower. This will leave room to add a single French Knot or several French Knots for the flower center.

WHIPPED BACKSTITCH

Wrapping a line of Backstitches with a different color thread makes interesting stems. If your stem turns out darker than you want, whip lighter colored thread over the Backstitching. Use a blunt pointed tapestry needle.

Work a line of Backstitches (Fig. 24).

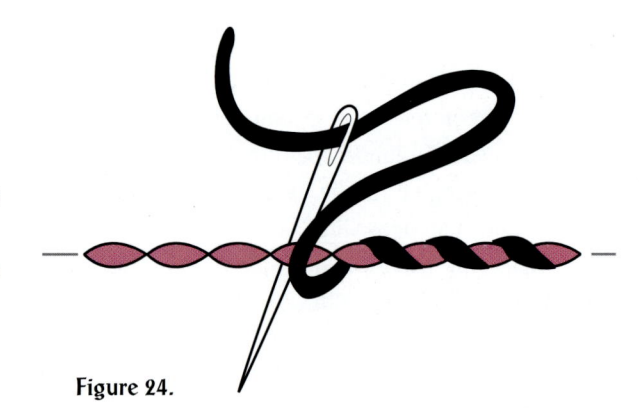

Figure 24.

Use a tapestry needle and contrasting thread.

Work over and under each Backstitch, sliding the needle under the thread, rather than through the fabric.

General Directions

The ribbons listed in the supply list are what were used in "Smitten with Flowers." If you wish to use a different color scheme, the supply list will help you purchase the amount of ribbon needed to complete the quilt.

A line drawing of each block is a placement diagram for the stems, leaves, and flowers. The only thing you need to draw on your background is the placement; do this by drawing a line the length of a leaf or petal, rather than drawing the outline of each leaf and petal.

Symbols are used to help you with the stitches. For instance, ◆ is the symbol for the Ribbon Stitch and it is shown in the diagrams each time the Ribbon Stitch is used.

The order of stitching, the stitches, and the ribbon or thread used are detailed for each of the nine blocks and the embroidered vine border. Remember, the blocks are stitched in the same order a flower grows – first the stems, the leaves, and finally the flowers.

Let the ribbon work for you to create dimension in the quilt. It takes a little practice, but try to make loose stitches, especially for the leaves and flower petals. Sometimes the ribbon wants to twist. You can use your fingers or thumb to help control the ribbon as you pull the ribbon through to the back of the quilt. A toothpick or your needle can be used to help straighten the ribbon as the stitches are formed. Slide the toothpick under the ribbon near the base of the stitch (Fig. 25).

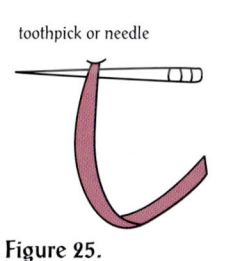

Figure 25.

Ribbons & Threads: Baltimore Style

15

The Blocks

BLOCK 1 – RUCHED ROSE
STITCHING ORDER
  Stems:
    Stem Stitch – single strand of green silk embroidery thread
  Leaves:
    Fly Stitch – 4mm variegated green silk ribbon
    Ribbon Stitch at the tip of each leaf section
  Rose:
    Ruched Rose – 4mm variegated red silk ribbon

Block 1.

16   Ribbons & Threads: Baltimore Style

BLOCK 2 – BERRY WREATH
STITCHING ORDER
  Stems:
    Stem Stitch – single strand of green silk embroidery thread
  Leaves:
    Lazy Daisy Stitch – 4mm variegated green silk ribbon
  Berries:
    Colonial Knots – 4mm variegated red silk ribbon

Block 2.

Ribbons & Threads: Baltimore Style

17

BLOCK 3 – EIGHT-PETAL ROSE WREATH

Stitching Order

Stems:
  Stem Stitch – single strand of green silk embroidery thread

Leaves:
  Ribbon Stitch – 4mm variegated green silk ribbon

Flowers:
  Ribbon Stitch – 4mm variegated violet/gold silk ribbon

Flower Centers:
  Straight Stitch – same ribbon as flowers

Block 3.

Ribbons & Threads: Baltimore Style

BLOCK 4 – CHERRY WREATH

Stitching Order

Stems:
　　Circle/Whipped Backstitch – backstitch circle with a single strand of green silk embroidery thread; whip the Backstitch with a single strand of a different green silk embroidery thread

Cherry stems:
　　Backstitch – single strand of green silk embroidery thread

Leaves:
　　Ribbon Stitch – 4mm variegated green silk ribbon

Cherries:
　　French Knots – single strand of red silk embroidery thread

Block 4.

Ribbons & Threads: Baltimore Style

BLOCK 5 – ROSE WREATH
Stitching Order
Stems:

Whipped Backstitch – backstitch circle with a single strand of green silk embroidery thread; whip the Backstitch with a single strand of a different green silk embroidery thread.

Leaves:

Ribbon Stitch – 7mm variegated green silk ribbon

Leaf Veins:

Running Stitch – single strand of lightest green silk embroidery thread

Roses:

Folded Roses – 7mm variegated blue/blue green silk ribbon, make eight roses

Block 5.

BLOCK 6 – WILD ROSE WREATH

Stitching Order

Stems:
  Coral Stitch – single strand of dark green silk embroidery thread

Leaves:
  Ribbon Stitch – 4mm variegated green silk ribbon

Wild Roses:
  Ribbon Stitch – 4mm variegated yellow/red orange silk ribbon

Rose Centers:
  Colonial Knots – single strand of white silk embroidery thread

Block 6.

Ribbons & Threads: Baltimore Style

BLOCK 7 – ROSE GARDEN WREATH
STITCHING ORDER
  Stems:
    Stem Stitch – single strand of green silk embroidery thread
  Rosebuds:
    Rosebuds – 4mm variegated violet/gold silk ribbon for the buds (Padded Ribbon Stitch)
  Leaves:
    Ribbon Stitch and Side Ribbon Stitch (for Rosebuds) – 4mm variegated green silk ribbon
  Roses:
    Edge-Gathered Rose – 4mm variegated violet/gold silk ribbon, make four roses
  Rose Centers:
    French Knots – single strand of gold silk embroidery thread

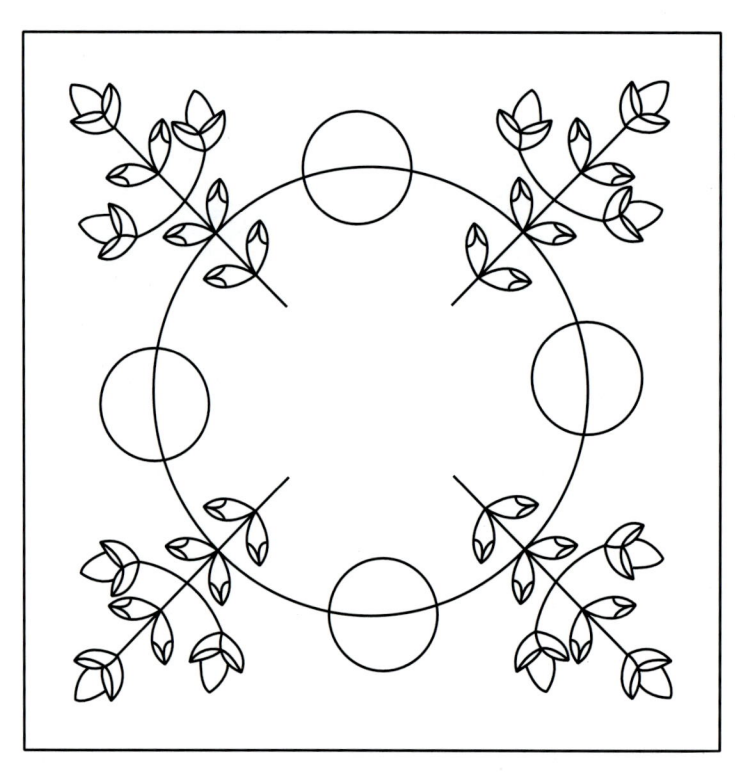

Block 7.

Ribbons & Threads: Baltimore Style

BLOCK 8 – HEART ROSEBUD WREATH
Stitching Order

Stems:
- Stem Stitch – single strand of green silk embroidery thread

Rosebuds:
- Rosebuds – 4mm variegated red silk ribbon for buds, 4mm variegated green silk ribbon for leaves

Leaves:
- Ribbon Stitch – 4mm variegated green silk ribbon

Rosebud Stems:
- Straight Stitch – single strand of green silk embroidery thread

Block 8.

Ribbons & Threads: Baltimore Style

BLOCK 9 – GRAPES & ROSES

STITCHING ORDER

Stems:
   Stem Stitch – single strand of green silk embroidery thread

Leaves:
   Ribbon Stitch – 4mm variegated green silk ribbon

Grapevines:
   Stem Stitch – single strand of sewing thread in brown (use several different colors)

Grapes:
   Colonial Knots – #8 purple perle cotton or two strands of purple silk embroidery thread

Roses:
   Center-Gathered Roses – 4mm variegated red silk ribbon, make eight roses

Block 9.

EMBROIDERED VINE BORDER

Stitching Order

Vines:
  Stem Stitch – single strand of green silk embroidery thread

Leaves:
  Ribbon Stitch – 4mm variegated green silk ribbon

Grapes:
  Colonial Knots – #8 purple perle cotton or two strands of purple silk embroidery thread

Roses in corners:
  Straight Stitch (make them very loose to give dimension to petals) – 4mm variegated red silk ribbon

Roses at center of each side:
  Center-Gathered Roses – 4mm variegated red silk ribbon, make four roses

Full-size pattern for one side is on page 26.

Bottom left corner of Embroidered Vine Border.

QUILTED FEATHER BORDER

Mark the quilting design onto the outer border. The disappearing ink fabric marker can be used if you intend to quilt it immediately, or use a very light pencil marking. A template can also be made from the design so you can mark it as you go, if you wish.

QUILTING THE BACKGROUND

Quilting thread to match the background fabric is used for the quilting. A ¼" grid has been stitched in the background behind the embroidered designs. This can be marked or you can use your eye to judge the spacing. Echo quilting is stitched in the Embroidered Vine border, spacing the lines ⅛" or less apart.

Full-size pattern for one side is on page 27.

Bottom left corner of Quilted Feather Border.

Ribbons & Threads: Baltimore Style

A - - - - B

Border should measure 13¼" for each side.

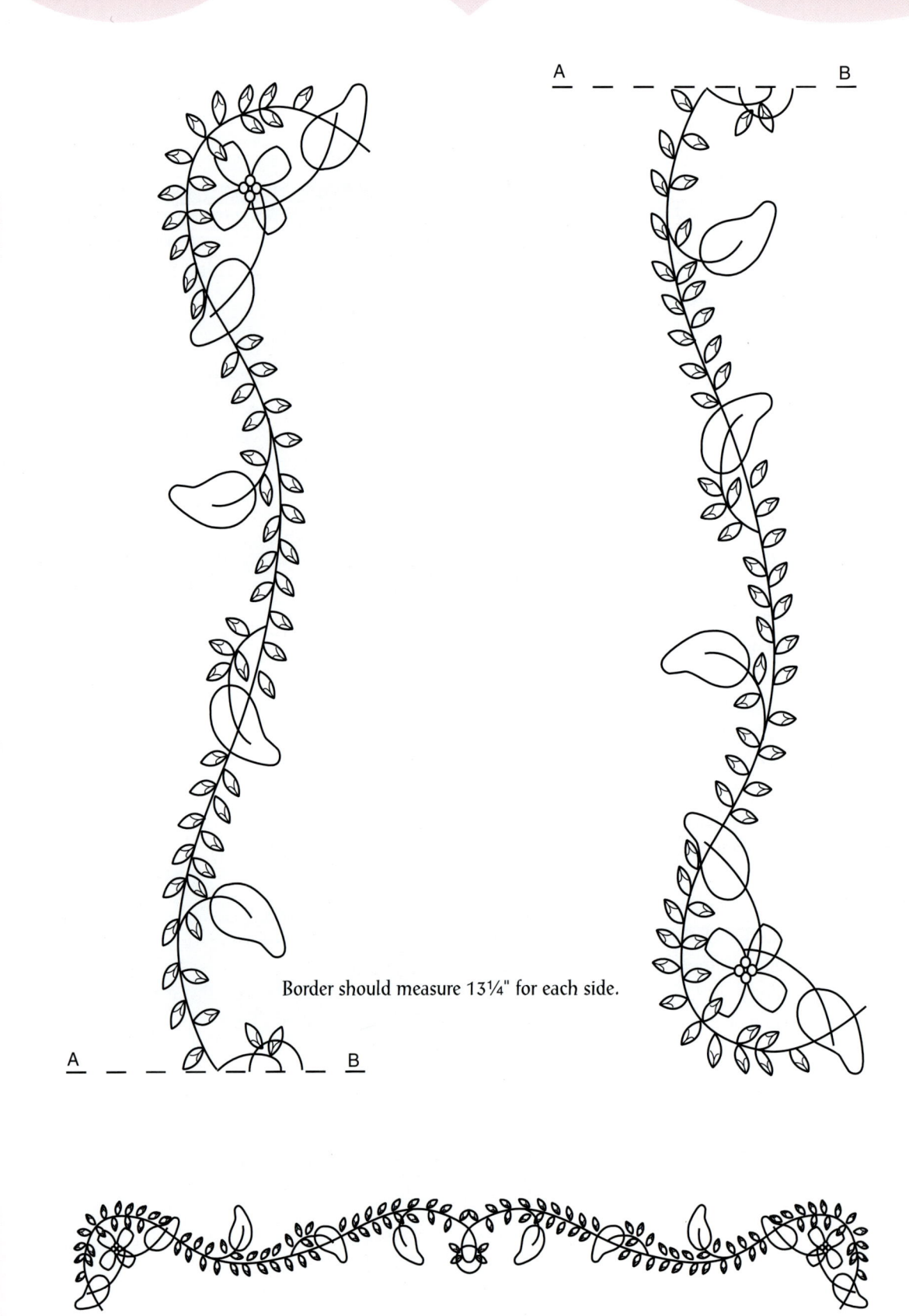

A - - - - B

One complete side, Embroidered Vine Border

26 Ribbons & Threads: Baltimore Style

Border should measure 16¼" for each side.

One complete side, Quilted Feather Border

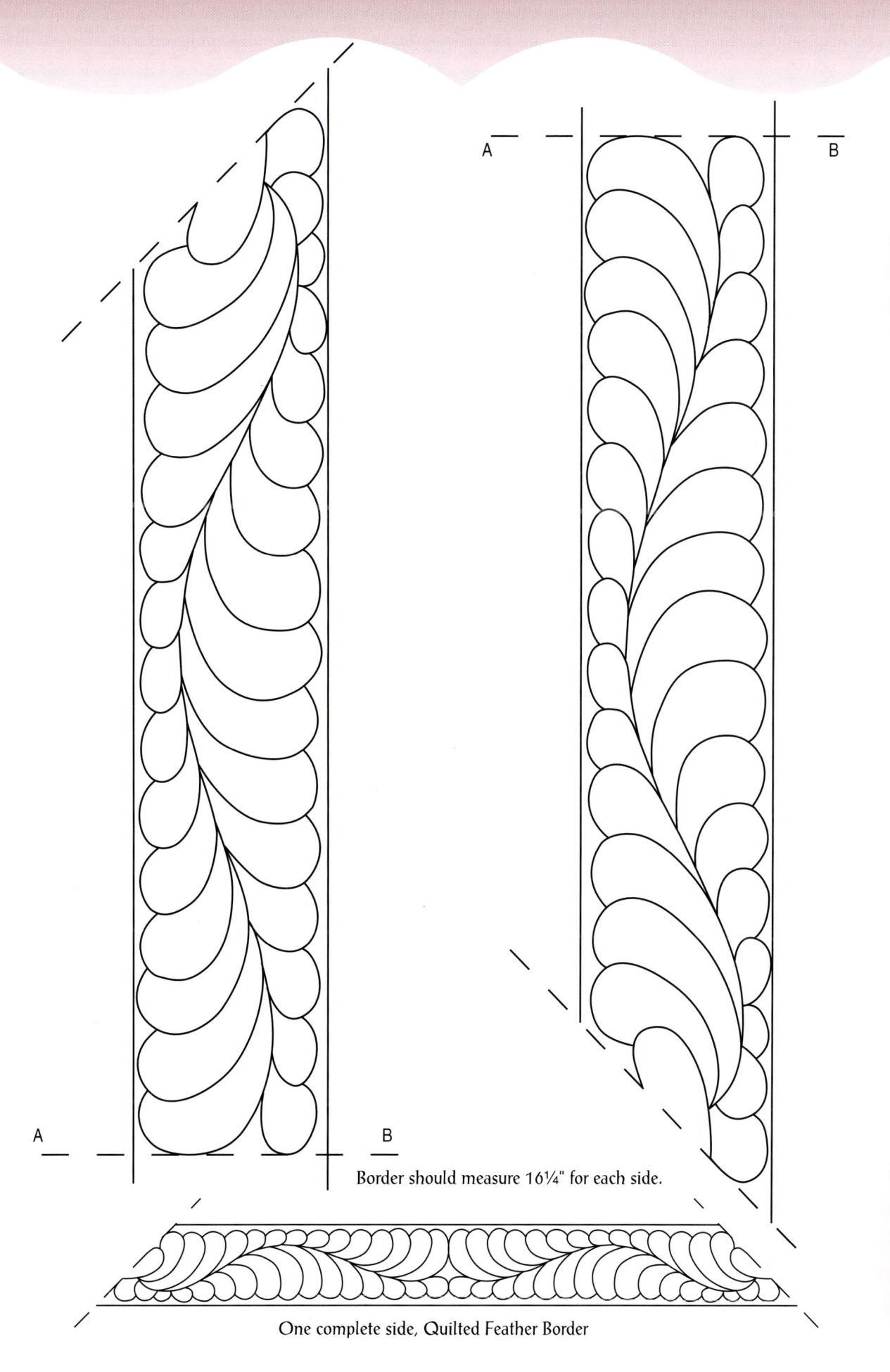

Ribbons & Threads: Baltimore Style

27

Ribbons & Threads: Baltimore Style

Finishing the Quilt

Prior to finishing a quilt, it is important to square up the edges and make sure the corners are 90°. Using a 6" ruler, lay the ruler on a straight line in the quilt – the Cable stitching in the border should be a good straight line. Measure across the Feathered Vine border and add ¼" seam allowance. Draw a line on your quilt along the edge of the ruler. Measure all four sides and mark in the same manner, making sure the corners are 90°. Using your rotary cutter or scissors, cut on the lines, removing the excess fabric.

Make your binding from a bias strip of background fabric, 1" x 65". Cut a 45° angle in one end with the strip laid out flat (Fig. 26). Fold the strip in half lengthwise, wrong sides together. Lay the raw edge of the binding (with the fold facing toward the center of the quilt) along the raw edge of the quilt, starting about 3" from a lower corner. Leave a 4" tail to aid in joining the ends when the binding has been stitched around the entire quilt.

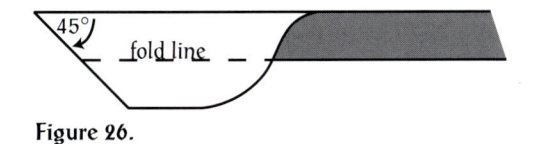

Figure 26.

Place a pin ¼" from the corner of the quilt. Begin stitching the binding, using a scant ¼" seam allowance (Fig. 27). Stitch until you reach the pin; take a couple of backstitches. Raise the presser foot and cut the threads.

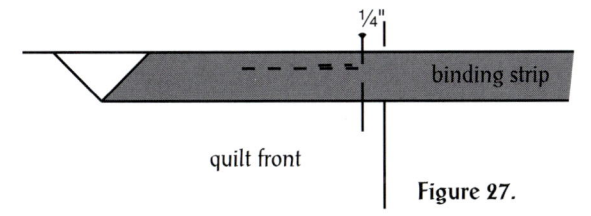

Figure 27.

Fold the binding up to form a 45° angle in the corner (Fig. 28). Next fold the binding down along the second edge, making sure the fold is even with the edge of the quilt at the corner (Fig. 29). Place a pin ¼" from the second corner. Begin stitching at the corner and continue until you come to the pin again; backstitch and cut the thread. Stitch the binding on the third side in the same manner. On the fourth side, start stitching from

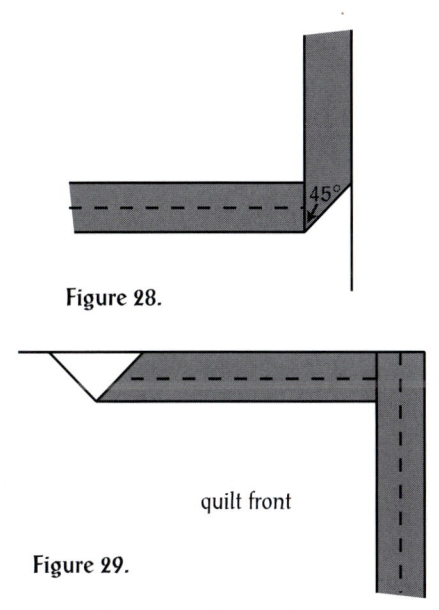

Figure 28.

Figure 29.

the corner and stop stitching when you are about 4" from where you started.

Lay the tail of the binding where you stopped along the raw edge of the quilt (Fig. 30). Now lay the edge of the miter you cut at the beginning over the top of the tail. Make a pencil mark where the edge of the miter starts. If we were to draw a miter on the tail end here, the two pieces would only meet. We need a seam allowance for both ends. From the pencil mark you made, place a second pencil mark ½" (that is two ¼" seam allowances) toward the end of the tail (Fig. 31, on page 30). Open the beginning miter out flat so you can see which direction the miter goes. Using that as a guide, place your ruler on the tail end to mark a miter in the same direction. Cut the excess binding off on the mitered line.

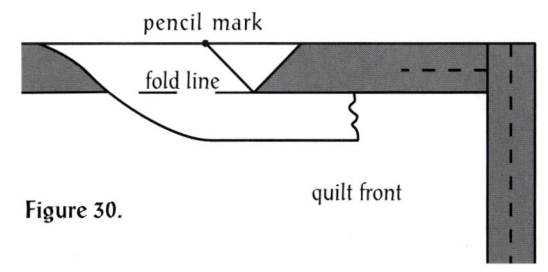

Figure 30.

Now with the binding opened flat, stitch the two mitered ends, right sides together, and finger press the seam allowance open. Fold the binding in half again

Ribbons & Threads: Baltimore Style

29

Figure 31.

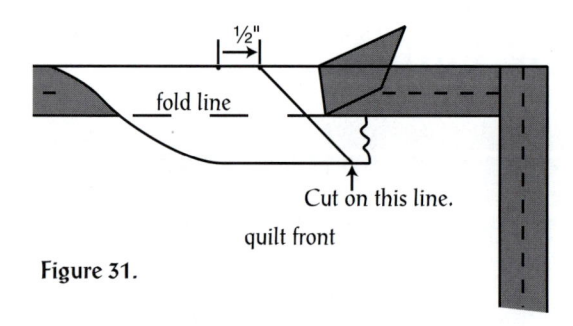

and stitch the remaining section to the quilt. Now, wasn't that easy? This method gives you a very neat finish to your binding.

After the binding has been stitched to the edge, Stem Stitch along the binding using a single strand of red silk embroidery thread (Fig. 32).

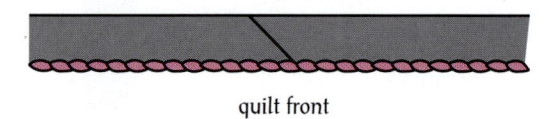

Figure 32.

Fold the binding over to the back side of the quilt and blindstitch it in place (Fig. 33). Make sure the stitching line is covered. Also remember to stitch the mitered corners closed on both the front and back of the quilt. An easy way to remember to do this is to stitch until you get to the corner, fold the mitered corner in place and take a tacking stitch at the base of the miter. Slide your needle through to the front and stitch along the miter to the corner; at the top, slide your needle to the back and stitch down the back of the miter. Continue blindstitching the binding.

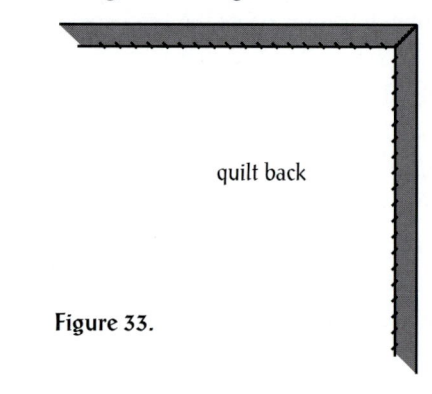

Figure 33.

Once you have completed the binding, you are ready to put a label with your name, city, state, date, and any other information you wish, on the back of your quilt.

And, finally, you can sit back and enjoy your quilt. May your Baltimore style silk ribbon quilt be a prize winner too!

References

The following references provide additional ideas for blocks and embroidery stitches that can be used in your own Baltimore style quilts in threads and ribbons.

Brown, Pauline, editor. **Embroidery.** New York, NY: Villard Books, a division of Random House, 1986.

Kolter, Jane Bentley. **Forget Me Not.** Pittstown, NJ: The Main Street Press, Inc., 1985.

Lane, Rose Wilder. **American Needlework.** New York, NY: Simon and Schuster, 1963.

McMorris, Penny. **Crazy Quilts.** New York, NY: Penguin Books USA Inc., 1984.

Montano, Judith Baker. **Elegant Stitches.** Lafayette, CA: C & T Publishing, 1995.

Nelson, Cyril I. and Carter Houck. **The Quilt Engagement Calendar Treasury.** New York, NY: E. P. Dutton, Inc., 1982.

Sienkiewicz, Elly. **Baltimore Beauties and Beyond.** Lafayette, CA: C & T Publishing, 1989.

West, Deanna Hall. **An Encyclopedia of Ribbon Embroidery Flowers.** San Marcos, CA: American School of Needlework, Inc., 1995.

SUPPLIERS:

Web of Thread
1410 Broadway
Paducah, KY 42001
1-800-955-8185
Ribbons & Threads

Quality HomeCraft Products
2255 NE Porter Rd.
Blue Springs, MO 64013
(816) 228-5550
No Slip Hoop

About the Author

Bonnie's mother taught her to sew as a child. She has been quilting since 1979, making her first quilt with blocks silk screened for an art class. Since that time she has enjoyed adding her own special elements to give traditional designs a new look. As a designer and artist, Bonnie enjoys using a variety of media and techniques.

Sharing her quilting knowledge, Bonnie conducts workshops for quilt groups and conferences across the country. She is a quilt judge, certified by NQA, and is qualified to judge master quilts. She is employed as Quilt Show Chairman at the American Quilter's Society, writes and edits books on quiltmaking.

Her quilts, wallhangings, and clothing have been shown in galleries, museums, and quilt shows, winning numerous awards. Her quilted works are in the Artists of Iowa Collection, Waterloo, Iowa; the Museum of the American Quilter's Society, Paducah, Kentucky; and private collections. Bonnie is included in the first edition of **Who's Who in American Quilting**, published by AQS, 1996.

She and her husband, Wayne, and White Sox, the cat, live in Paducah, Kentucky.

AQS Books on Quilts

This is only a partial listing of the books on quilts that are available from the American Quilter's Society. AQS books are known the world over for their timely topics, clear writing, beautiful color photographs, and accurate illustrations and patterns. Most of the following books are available from your local bookseller, quilt shop, or public library. If you are unable to locate certain titles in your area, you may order by mail from the AMERICAN QUILTER'S SOCIETY, P.O. Box 3290, Paducah, KY 42002-3290. Customers with Visa or MasterCard may phone in orders from 7:00–4:00 CST, Monday–Friday, Toll Free 1-800-626-5420. Add $2.00 for postage for the first book ordered and $0.40 for each additional book. Include item number, title, and price when ordering. Allow 14 to 21 days for delivery.

#	Title	Price
4595	Above & Beyond Basics, Karen Kay Buckley	$18.95
2282	Adapting Architectural Details for Quilts, Carol Wagner	$12.95
1907	American Beauties: Rose & Tulip Quilts, Marston & Cunningham	$14.95
4543	American Quilt Blocks: 50 Patterns for 50 States, Beth Summers	$16.95
4696	Amish Kinder Komforts, Betty Havig	$14.95
2121	Appliqué Designs: My Mother Taught Me to Sew, Faye Anderson	$12.95
3790	Appliqué Patterns from Native American Beadwork Designs, Dr. Joyce Mori	$14.95
2122	The Art of Hand Appliqué, Laura Lee Fritz	$14.95
2099	Ask Helen: More About Quilting Designs, Helen Squire	$14.95
2207	Award-Winning Quilts: 1985-1987	$24.95
2354	Award-Winning Quilts: 1988-1989	$24.95
3425	Award-Winning Quilts: 1990-1991	$24.95
3791	Award-Winning Quilts: 1992-1993	$24.95
4593	Blossoms by the Sea: Making Ribbon Flowers for Quilts, Faye Labanaris	$24.95
4697	Caryl Bryer Fallert: A Spectrum of Quilts, 1983-1995, Caryl Bryer Fallert	$24.95
3926	Celtic Style Floral Appliqué, Scarlett Rose	$14.95
2208	Classic Basket Quilts, Elizabeth Porter & Marianne Fons	$16.95
2355	Creative Machine Art, Sharee Dawn Roberts	$24.95
4818	Dear Helen, Can You Tell Me? Helen Squire	$15.95
3870	Double Wedding Ring Quilts: New Quilts from an Old Favorite	$14.95
3399	Dye Painting! Ann Johnston	$19.95
2030	Dyeing & Overdyeing of Cotton Fabrics, Judy Mercer Tescher	$9.95
4814	Encyclopedia of Designs for Quilting, Phyllis D. Miller	$34.95
3468	Encyclopedia of Pieced Quilt Patterns, compiled by Barbara Brackman	$34.95
3846	Fabric Postcards, Judi Warren	$22.95
4594	Firm Foundations: Techniques & Quilt Blocks for Precision Piecing, Jane Hall & Dixie Haywood	$18.95
2356	Flavor Quilts for Kids to Make, Jennifer Amor	$12.95
2381	From Basics to Binding, Karen Kay Buckley	$16.95
4526	Gatherings: America's Quilt Heritage, Kathlyn F. Sullivan	$34.95
2097	Heirloom Miniatures, Tina M. Gravatt	$9.95
4628	Helen's Guide to quilting in the 21st century, Helen Squire	$16.95
2120	The Ins and Outs: Perfecting the Quilting Stitch, Patricia J. Morris	$9.95
1906	Irish Chain Quilts: A Workbook of Irish Chains, Joyce B. Peaden	$14.95
3784	Jacobean Appliqué: Book I, "Exotica," Patricia B. Campbell & Mimi Ayars, Ph.D	$18.95
4544	Jacobean Appliqué: Book II, "Romantica," Patricia B. Campbell & Mimi Ayars, Ph.D	$18.95
3904	The Judge's Task: How Award-Winning Quilts Are Selected, Patricia J. Morris	$19.95
4751	Liberated Quiltmaking, Gwen Marston	$24.95
4523	Log Cabin Quilts: New Quilts from an Old Favorite	$14.95
4545	Log Cabin with a Twist, Barbara T. Kaempfer	$18.95
4815	Love to Quilt: Bears, Bears, Bears, Karen Kay Buckley	$14.95
4598	Love to Quilt: Men's Vests, Alexandra Capadalis Dupré	$14.95
4753	Love to Quilt: Penny Squares, Willa Baranowski	$12.95
2206	Marbling Fabrics for Quilts, Kathy Fawcett & Carol Shoaf	$12.95
4752	Miniature Quilts: Connecting New & Old Worlds, Tina M. Gravatt	$14.95
4514	Mola Techniques for Today's Quilters, Charlotte Patera	$18.95
3330	More Projects and Patterns: A Second Collection of Favorite Quilts, Judy Florence	$18.95
1981	Nancy Crow: Quilts and Influences, Nancy Crow	$29.95
3331	Nancy Crow: Work in Transition, Nancy Crow	$12.95
3332	New Jersey Quilts – 1777 to 1950: Contributions to an American Tradition, The Heritage Quilt Project of New Jersey	$29.95
3927	New Patterns from Old Architecture, Carol Wagner	$12.95
2153	No Dragons on My Quilt, Jean Ray Laury	$12.95
4627	Ohio Star Quilts: New Quilts from an Old Favorite	$16.95
3469	Old Favorites in Miniature, Tina Gravatt	$15.95
4515	Paint and Patches: Painting on Fabrics with Pigment, Vicki L. Johnson	$18.95
3333	A Patchwork of Pieces: An Anthology of Early Quilt Stories 1845 – 1940, complied by Cuesta Ray Benberry and Carol Pinney Crabb	$14.95
4513	Plaited Patchwork, Shari Cole	$19.95
3928	Precision Patchwork for Scrap Quilts, Jeannette Tousley Muir	$12.95
4779	Protecting Your Quilts: A Guide for Quilt Owners, Second Edition	$6.95
4542	A Quilted Christmas, edited by Bonnie Browning	$18.95
2380	Quilter's Registry, Lynne Fritz	$9.95
3467	Quilting Patterns from Native American Designs, Dr. Joyce Mori	$12.95
3470	Quilting with Style: Principles for Great Pattern Design, Marston & Cunningham	$24.95
2284	Quiltmaker's Guide: Basics & Beyond, Carol Doak	$19.95
2257	Quilts: The Permanent Collection – MAQS	$9.95
3793	Quilts: The Permanent Collection – MAQS Volume II	$9.95
3789	Roots, Feathers & Blooms: 4-Block Quilts, Their History & Patterns, Book I, Linda Carlson	$16.95
4512	Sampler Quilt Blocks from Native American Designs, Dr. Joyce Mori	$14.95
3796	Seasons of the Heart & Home: Quilts for a Winter's Day, Jan Patek	$18.95
3761	Seasons of the Heart & Home: Quilts for Summer Days, Jan Patek	$18.95
2357	Sensational Scrap Quilts, Darra Duffy Williamson	$24.95
3375	Show Me Helen…How to Use Quilting Designs, Helen Squire	$15.95
4783	Silk Ribbons by Machine, Jeanie Sexton	$15.95
1790	Somewhere in Between: Quilts and Quilters of Illinois, Rita Barrow Barber	$14.95
3794	Spike & Zola: Patterns Designed for Laughter…and Appliqué, Painting, or Stenciling, Donna French Collins	$9.95
3929	The Stori Book of Embellishing, Mary Stori	$16.95
3903	Straight Stitch Machine Appliqué, Letty Martin	$16.95
3792	Striplate Piecing: Piecing Circle Designs with Speed and Accuracy, Debra Wagner	$24.95
3930	Tessellations & Variations: Creating One-Patch and Two-Patch Quilts, Barbara Ann Caron	$14.95
3788	Three-Dimensional Appliqué and Embroidery Embellishment: Techniques for Today's Album Quilt, Anita Shackelford	$24.95
4596	Ties, Ties, Ties: Traditional Quilts from Neckties, Janet B. Elwin	$19.95
3931	Time-Span Quilts: New Quilts from Old Tops, Becky Herdle	$16.95
2029	A Treasury of Quilting Designs, Linda Goodmon Emery	$14.95
3847	Tricks with Chintz: Using Large Prints to Add New Magic to Traditional Quilt Blocks, Nancy S. Breland	$14.95
2286	Wonderful Wearables: A Celebration of Creative Clothing, Virginia Avery	$24.95